"SIMPLIFIED TRADING SKILLS"

(Very Easy To................

Comprehend Strategies)

CONTENTS

- Introduction

- How To Identify A Trend & Determine The Health Status

- The Importance of Considering Fundamental News Release

- Checking Longer Time Frames

- Price Patterns

- Main Level of Support/Resistance

- Price Action Script

- Stop-Loss & Target

- Time Scope

- Minimizing Risk While Generating Cash-Flow/Profit(s) From The Market(s)

- Appendix

INTRODUCTION

The world's economy largely runs on foreign exchange (forex), a market that accounts for an average trade volume worth over $5.3 trillion(USD) daily.

In many ways, the FX market is considered the largest amongst others.

More specifically, there are certain fundamentals (i.e ranging from...demand for/and supply of goods & services both internationally and domestically, interest rate decisions, inflation data, employment/unemployment data, geopolitical risk(s), just to mention a few) and some valid technicals (i.e trend analysis, and the like) that could impact a nation's economy either positively or negatively, as well as going further to determine the current market value of its currency.

That said, you may also want to read through this economic news>>>(https://l.facebook.com/l.php?u=https%3A%2F%2Fwww.forextime.com%2Fmarket-analysis%2Fdollar-suffers-unexpectedly-weak-nfp%3Futm_source%3Dnewsletter%26utm_medium%3Demail%26utm_content%3Dread-more-btn%26utm_campaign%3Dmarket-analysis-gl&h=ATOwr7BkpUpwfGA4l6mdavdQEU_06BAls3lxZBKyEbe9yleDCC37yxJwAVBLA6Q2VVvBe6x7emd6OdvUG556dah2RtdssNFhwYAq3fUk6UrTMXYli2MD9F2xePGbYm1z560FaUgy61sR) to have a glimpse of how certain fundamentals could impact positively or negatively on a currency.

Chapter One:

HOW TO IDENTIFY A TREND & DETERMINE THE HEALTH STATUS

Whilst it's important and advisable to be a trend trader....(trading in the direction of the main trend or overall market sentiment), it is also paramount to determine the health status of the trending setup(s) you're looking to trade.

It may be so easy to identify a trend...(i.e when price candles' keep making 'higher-highs' and 'higher-lows' if it were in an up-trend, or 'lower-highs' and 'lower-lows' if it were in a down-trend), but it is not that easy to determine its' health status; telling whether or not such trend is still "healthy" (nicely trending) or "unhealthy" (experiencing some form of early weakness and about to fissile out)!

Howbeit, the good news is this; By simply applying the following six(6) conditions to read price action around the 3~simple moving average(s); marked in green>(the 30SMA), red>(the 50SMA), and blue>(the 100SMA)!,,,,,,,,,"You'll literally be able to determine the health status of a trend. (Make reference to the attached snapshots showing the simple moving averages)!

#uptrending setup_____downtrending setup#

__3~SMAs__

__Highs'__

__Lows'__

That said, the six(6) different conditions are;

1) All 3~SMAs are in order..(i.e meaning the 30SMA is above the 50SMA, and the 50SMA is above the 100SMA...if it were in an up-trend) or (the 30SMA is below the 50SMA, and the 50SMA is below the 100SMA...if it were in a down-trend)!

2) All 3~SMAs points in the same direction...(beit up-trending or down-trending setups)!

3) All 3~SMAs are parallel to each other...(meaning; no crossover between them)!

4) Price remains/held above or on the left side of the 50SMA≥(the SMA in middle; marked in red) if it were in an up-trend or below/on the right side of the 50SMA...if it were in a down-trend!

5) Price no-where near the 100SMA...(meaning; price mustn't come close or touch the 100SMA marked in blue)!

6) Harmonic swings__off/or between the 30/50 SMA area...(meaning; price candles should touch, occur from, or swing off the area between the 30/50 simple moving average(s), and it should swing off in the direction of the main trend or overall market sentiment)!

Going forward, with all the six(6) different conditions nicely or wrongly playing out around the 3~SMAs, you could easily determine the health status of any trending setup, regardless of the market(s) or instrument(s) you trade;

Beit [Forex (fiat currencies), Stocks, Cryptos, Commodities (gold, silver, crude oil, natural gas, etc) and many other investment instruments traded live on the markets]

More specifically, when you scroll down and closely look into the photo snapshots of "EUR/JPY, AUD/CAD, USD/JPY, GBP/CAD, and GBP/CHF currency pair(s); you'll see how the afore mentioned six(6) conditions nicely played out around the 3~SMAs, and as you analyze and trade with those six(6) conditions in place, chances are that you're looking to trade high probability setups, yielding more and more profits in the bank...(your portfolio in this case)!

Also, when you closely look into the photo snapshots of "GBP/USD" currency pair, you'll notice some early signs of weakness around the 3~SMAs; the 30SMA>(the SMA in green) is beginning to flatten, no longer pointing down>(which is the direction of the main trend or overall market sentiment); the 30SMA is also about to crossover the 50SMA, which already violates some or probably all of the six(6) conditions mentioned earlier.

And thereafter, in the second snapshot of the same "GBP/USD" pair, you could see the catastrophic loss that would have happen to any "bearish" trader/investor attempting to search for a short opportunity at that junction of the chart.

Likewise in the photo snapshot of "CHF/JPY" pair, you could also see at the ranging/or top most part of the chart; how that price completely violates the entire six(6) conditions to lookout for...around the 3≈simple moving average(s).

So when you can control your emotions, consider and apply the afore mentioned six(6) conditions to your daily trade plan, and you'll eventually become a successful trader in the long run; trading at low risk, with high returns/profits!

Going forward, maybe at some point you may have thought "trading" is complex, and full of super-complicated concepts, but that isn't the reality..."when you know exactly...what and what not to lookout for"!

Now Carefully Relate The Information You've Read Above With The Photo Snapshots Below

The following snapshots represents' the information explained above;

i) Snapshots of 'EUR/JPY, AUD/CAD, USD/JPY, GBP/CAD, and GBP/CHF' Currency Pair(s)...respectively!

Level of Support

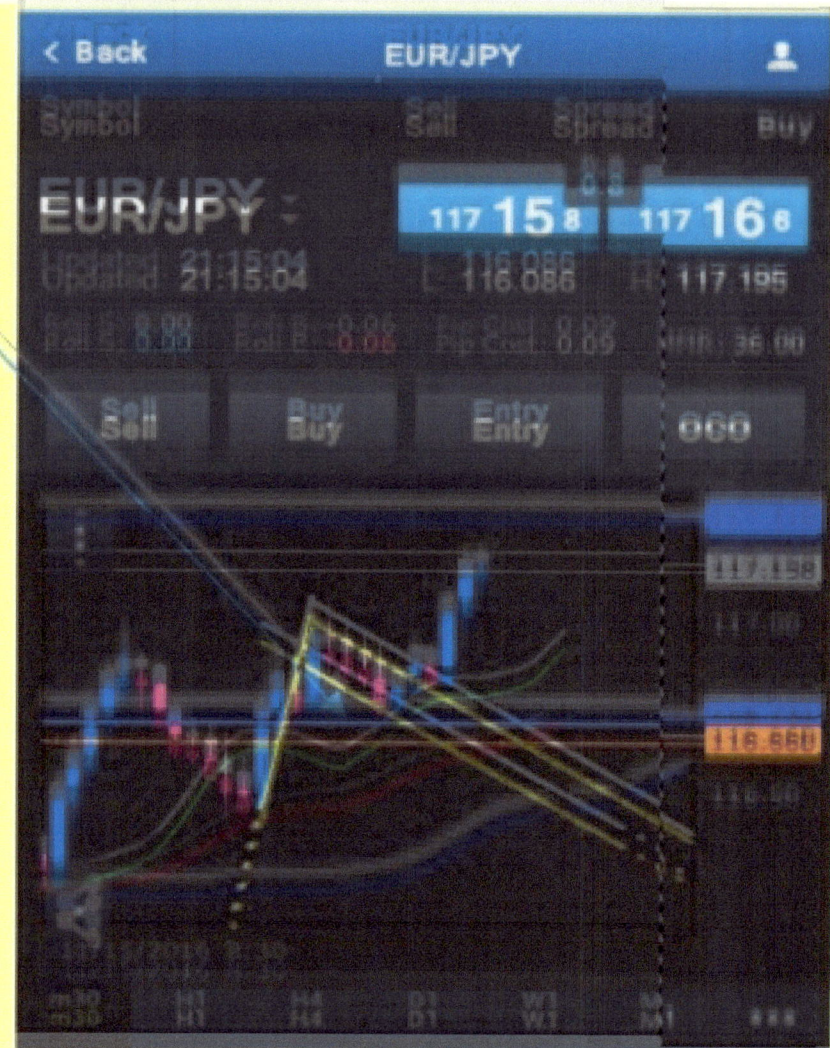

Level of Resistance

Fibonacci

(M) Reversal

Formation

(W) Reversal Formation

Retracement Trend Line(s)

Triangular Pattern (Flat-Bottom Triangle)

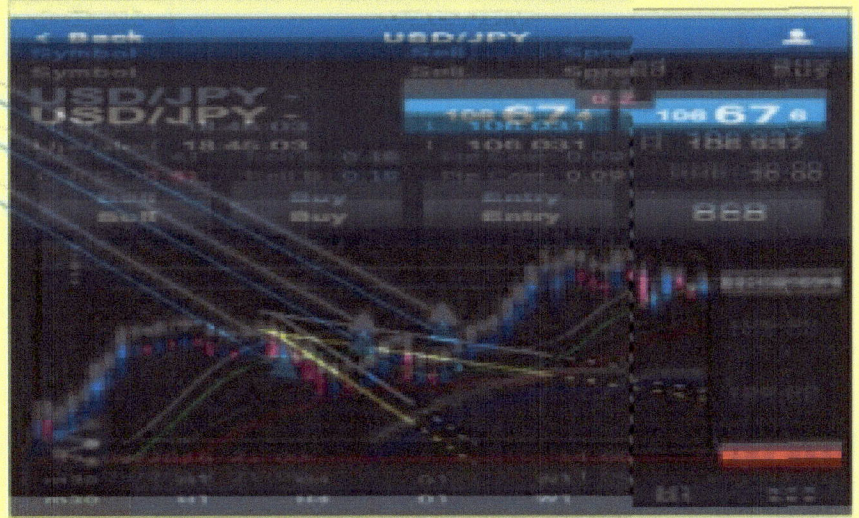

ii) Snapshots of 'GBP/USD' Currency Pair...(Both first & second Snapshots, as explained above)!

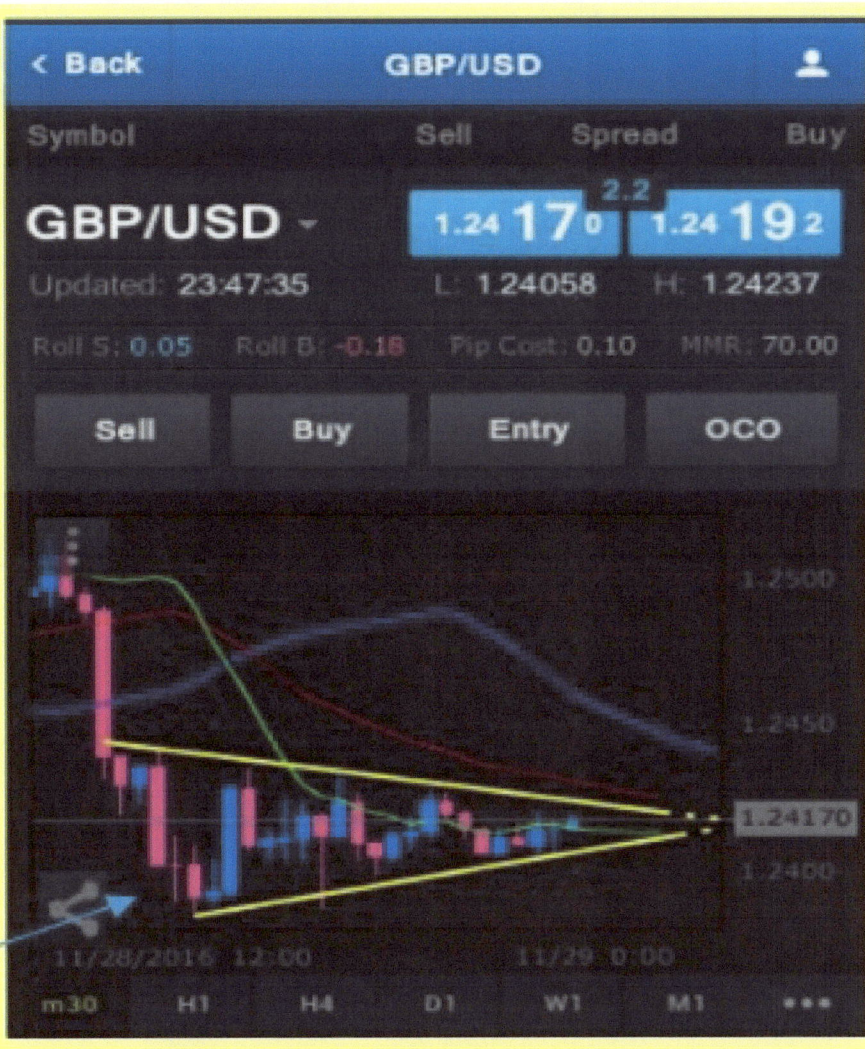

Triangular Pattern:-

(Regular Triangle)

iii) Snapshot of 'CHF/JPY' Currency Pair...(As explained above)!

Ranging Setup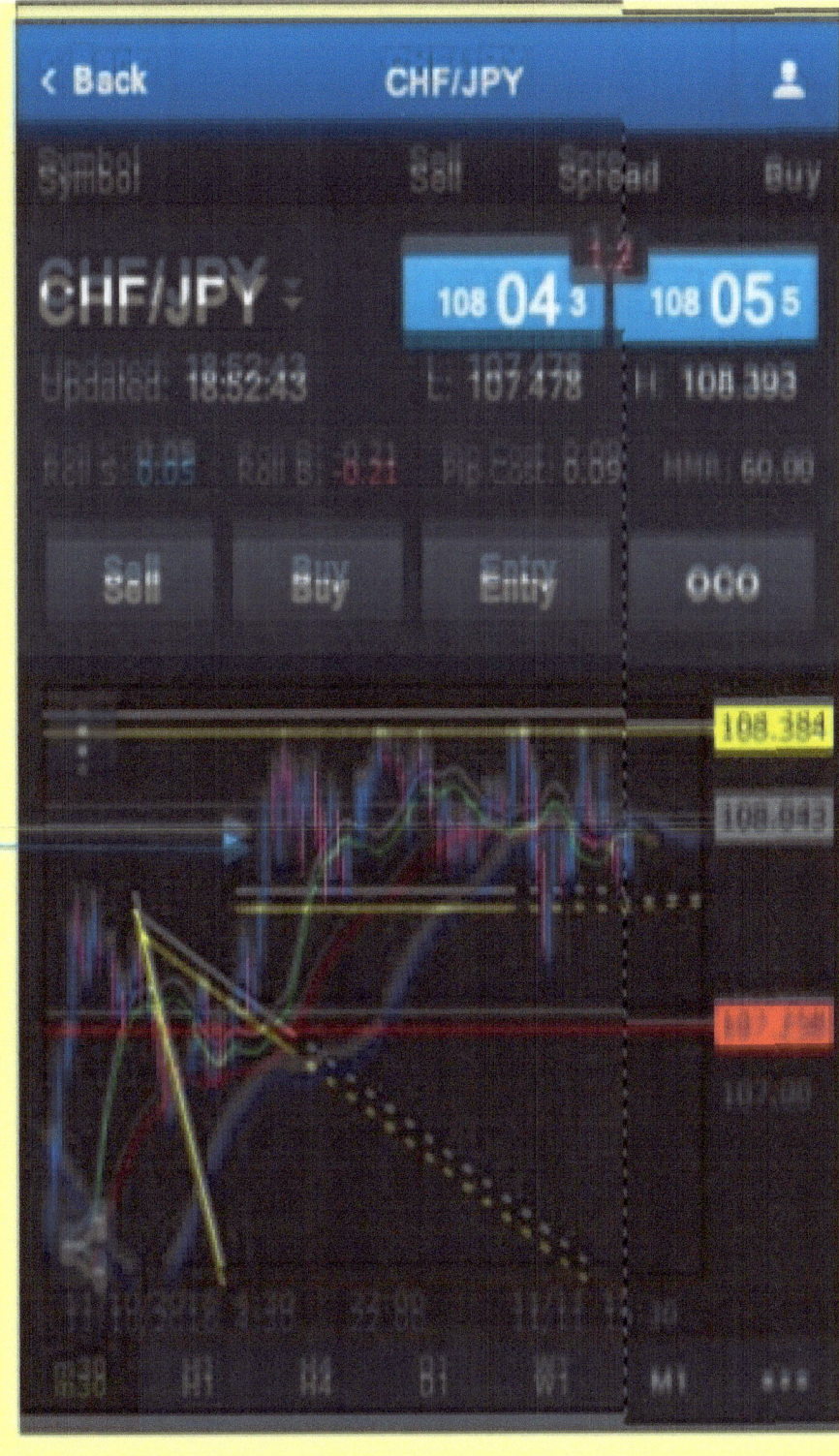

Chapter Two:

CONSIDERING ECONOMIC NEWS RELEASE

Having gone through the process of identifying a trend and determining its health status, the next best thing to do is to check your economic calender for any possible news release.

Now suppose you're looking to trade a currency pair, say (GBP/USD) for instance, always ensure to check whether or not there's an economic news coming around the time you're looking to trade that currency pair.

Why? Because it is not advisable to trade any pair at the precise time you noticed there's a fundamental news release coming on either one or both members of that pair, in order to avoid any random-spike in price to an unpredictable direction as a result of high, medium, or low volatility news release.

Infact, i even recommend not to trade such a pair 2-hours prior the news, but trade 30-minutes after the news.

On the other hand, if there's no economic news coming on both members of a pair as at the time you're looking to trade, then you could go ahead to trade such a pair.

To check for economic news release, kindly log on to (www.forexfactory.com)!

Chapter Three:
CHECKING LONGER TIME FRAMES

There are basically nine(9) common time frames...(i.e 1m, 5m, 30m, 1H, 4H, Daily or D1, Weekly or W1, Monthly or M1) as labelled by most charting platforms or brokerage firms.

However, I personally do trade from an intra-day perspective...(meaning I usually focus on the 30m, 1H, or 4Hours charts) and sometimes the Daily(D1) chart or time frame.

Meanwhile, I usually pay little or no attention to the 1minute or 5minutes time frames, especially when searching for nicely trending setups to trade.

Howbeit, every trader is free to decide the time frame(s) that best suits their individual trading personality and approach.

More specifically, it is very important to check longer time frames such as the Daily, Weekly, or Monthly charts...before taking an entry position on shorter time frames such as 1m, 5m, 30m, 1H, or even the 4H chart.

This may also help to reduce your risk, increase the odds in your favour, and as well save any potential loss that could arise from conflicting signals between the longer and shorter time frames.

(i.e your 3~SMA indicator pointing at different directions on both time frames, or having current market price on shorter time frames approach a long-term Support/Resistance level)!

Chapter Four:
PRICE PATTERNS

More often than not, I personally do trade swinging price formation in the direction of the main trend or overall market sentiment.

Kindly make reference to those photo snapshots I used earlier on while explaining how to identify a trend and determine its health status:

In addition, I also do trade breakouts (i.e triangles, ranging setups/channels) and reversal price formation in the direction of the main trend.

Chapter Five:

MAIN LEVEL

OF SUPPORT/RESISTANCE

The term 'support' is a line or level of defence which do apply when you're looking to trade setup(s) in an up-trending scenario or market condition.

While 'resistance' is also a level of defence but obviously do apply to down-trending scenerio(s) or market condition(s).

Meanwhile, to determine levels of support/resistance, it is paramount to consider or watchout for an area of confluence where certain elements of support/resistance converge or meet.

Examples of such elements are; trend line, counter trend line, fibonacci retracement (usually 38.2%, 50%, or 61.8% measurement), previous levels of support/resistance, previous breakout levels, and round numbers (00 and 50).

For instance, when you scroll back and closely look into the snapshot of "EUR/JPY" pair, you could see at price level (116.711), the blue horizontal line acted as support to price candles, thereby preventing price from breaching through to the downside.

Likewise, when you closely look into the snapshot of "AUD/CAD" pair, you could also see at price level (0.98798), the red horizontal line around the (38.2% fibonacci) partly acted as resistance to price candles, thereby preventing price from moving to the upward direction.

That said, it's important to also note that price candles obviously do react off these levels of support/resistance, with the possibility of price moving either to the upside, downside, or probably go sideways in a range.

Whichever direction price choose to go, always check to confirm whether or not those six(6) conditions as mentioned earlier...are still in place.

If they're not, then you do not want to search for any trading opportunity on such pair and time frame, at least for the meantime.

Chapter Six:

PRICE ACTION SCRIPT

Being a trend trader, I usually do wait to see price candles(beit bullish or bearish) reversing or turning in the direction of the overall market sentiment/trend...(beit up or down) upon hitting or approaching my main level of support/resistance.

You may also want to make reference to those snapshots I did mention earlier on, in order to see and carefully study how price candles are likely to behave or react.

Chapter Seven:
STOP-LOSS & TARGET

The term 'stop loss' defines how much stake you're willing to risk in a particular trade. While 'target' level(s) defines your exit strategy or how you intend to close your open trade(s), hopefully with a gain or profit.

As a conservative trader, it is pretty okay to keep a tight stop loss level, whenever possible, usually few pips or points below (if it were in an up trend)/above (if it were in a down trend) your strongest or main level of support/resistance.

Target level(s) in swinging price formation is usually determined by measuring the previous swing, and then project the measured swing-pole length from the area (i.e your main level of S/R) where price may likely reverse or turn in the direction of the main trend or overall market sentiment...(beit up or down).

Also make reference to those photo snapshots in order to have a clear view of the underlying subject matter.

Chapter Eight:

TIME SCOPE

This defines how long you intend to leave a trade open in hopes of price reaching your set target or before you manually close the trade(s).

Howbeit, from an intra-day and conservative perspective, it is pretty okay to leave a trade open on a 30m time frame for atmost 6-12hours, 1H for atmost 22-24hours, 4H for atmost 48hours, the Daily(D1) for atmost 7-10days, the Weekly(W1) for atmost 21days, to allow price candles unfold, given that every other conditions to lookout for are still in place and not yet violated.

Chapter Nine:

MINIMIZING RISK WHILE PROFITING

Every smart and conservative trader understands the dynamics of trading as well as market imperfections.

Due to this awareness, it is very important to have a solid trade plan before and after you trigger an entry button or position for a trade.

That said, by following and reading price action in real-time, carrying out in-trade management (checking to see whether or not price candles make new lows/highs in the direction of the overall market sentiment), tightening your stop loss level, or probably moving/trailing stop to breakeven, or hopefully cashing out all or half of your lot size in a trade, whichever way; you're better off in a position to minimizing risk and perhaps increasing the odds in your favour.

APPENDIX

As it regards government mismanagement of the money supply—(also known as 'fiat' currency), smart investors more often than not, do consider a venerable commodity such as gold—(A viable member of the precious metal family); as a safe haven over the centuries, based on certain fundamental and technical analysis being carried out:

In conclusion, however, it is not the investment vehicle, instrument, or product that is necessarily safe or risky, it is the investor.

Definition of Terms:

1) Bullish Candle(s):- Price candle(s) indicating an upward move.

2) Bearish Candle(s):- Price candle(s) indicating a downward move.

3) Bullish Investor:- An investor with the view of price going up.

4) **Bearish Investor:-** An investor with the view of price going down.

5) **Trend Line:-** A line drawn or projected to trace the direction and pattern of price.

6) **Counter Trend Line:-** A line that points in opposite direction to the main trend.

7) Fibonacci:= A technical trading tool that measures the retracement level of price candle(s).

8) Previous Breakout Levels:= Price levels that once acted as either support or resistance, but now act as resistance or support respectively.

9) Round Numbers:= This bespeaks numbers that ends with either (00) or (50).

P.S - Ensure to review all of the information communicated so you could gain accurate understanding.

That said, as the course progresses (after you might have signed up/made payment for the live session) you'll get to see more of practicals in video format, and as well learn more about investing and electronic trading skills.

For enquiries, kindly;

➢ Send an e-mail request - to (earnprudently994@gmail.com)!

➢ Call/whatsapp - (+2348172684450, +2348135343126)!

THE END

Production (C) 2018

@ Earn Prudently

www.ingramcontent.com/pod-product-compliance
Lightning Source LLC
Chambersburg PA
CBHW051924210526
45473CB00006B/2132